Woman Who am I

MAME YAA

ISBN 978-1-95081-808-2 (paperback)

Copyright © 2019 by Mame Yaa

All rights reserved. No part of this publication may be reproduced, distributed, or transmitted in any form or by any means, including photocopying, recording, or other electronic or mechanical methods without the prior written permission of the publisher. For permission requests, solicit the publisher via the address below.

Rushmore Press LLC
1 888 733 9607
www.rushmorepress.com

Scripture quotations marked KJV are from the Holy Bible, King James Version (Authorized Version). First published in 1611. Quoted from the KJV Classic Reference Bible, Copyright © 1983 by Zondervan Corporation.

Scripture quotations marked NIV are taken from the Holy Bible, New International Version®. Copyright © 1973, 1978, 1984 by International Bible Society. Used by permission of Zondervan. All rights reserved. [Biblica]

Contents

Acknowledgements 5

One—Introduction 7

Two—Woman of Substance 11

Three—Woman as a Wife 22

Four 34

Five—Participating Actively 38

Six—Woman as a Mother 41

Seven 45

Bonus Chapter 47

Acknowledgements

Special thanks to our Lord Jesus Christ who loves us all and created us as women for the world. Thanks to my mother, husband and kids for their indirect help which influenced me in writing this book. Thanks to my colleagues at work and to my human resource personnel Mrs. Beverly Stone who encouraged me to keep writing and Teresa Boleyjack who always proof read and add to my books. Thanks to all my lovely readers as well and God richly bless you for allowing yourselves to be a part of good change for the world.

One

Introduction

God gave special abilities to a woman which makes her able to do multiple things at a time without giving up. These abilities enable her to last through any situation and difficulties and through that she emerges as a champion for herself and others. Protective abilities, foresight, nurturing, these are but to name a few. Power to love which is one of her abilities enable her to endure and bring change around her. A woman is able to bring great change in the life of a prideful man because she is able to see beauty in that arrogant person that no one can see and therefore bring about change. This ability or power can be used for good or evil. These three people in the bible give us more insight on how the ability or the substance God gave them was used for bad.

The power of Delilah with Samson; he could kill thousands with a jawbone but he fell under the power of one woman. She used her power of beauty to fool a man for money and his destruction.

King David who killed goliath fell under the power of Bathsheba; she used her beauty to seduced a man of God and lost her husband in the process

King Solomon the wisest king who ruled over Israel married 700 wives and 300 concubines; they influenced him into turning away from God to the other gods.

I realized that nowadays, women are used for seduction purposes as form of sexual appeal to attract products sales. Mostly, seductive women are used for these purposes to attract men and others to buy their products. This power when not used well can be very deadly but that was not what God intended for us but to bring life and complete our partners and surroundings. Instead of using this form of seduction to destroy, we can use our complete sense of attractiveness to draw people to God. We can also use these means, (billboards, magazines etc. as a channel of showing how powerful God is.

Women are a special gift from the Lord such that when GOD had created all things and thought it was good and perfect; he knew something was missing from his creation. Then he realized it was a woman, for it was not good for a man to live alone. After God had created a woman and given special features to a woman to reflect God's own artistic abilities, God then saw that everything was perfect and he never created anything again.

Every woman is special and wonderful in the sight of God and man. It takes a woman to be able to understand the perfect creation of God.

In proverbs 3:14-18, proverbs 4:6-8; wisdom is attributed to a woman therefore it is expected of every woman to at least be wise in her sayings, actions and general life.

Two

Woman of Substance

This is a woman of power, of positive influence and a woman of significance (sense). To be branded a woman of substance is one of the greatest compliments one can get.

To be an influential woman, you need to have

- Sturdy character
- Interesting to get to know
- Own depth of personality and character.

MAME YAA

STURDY CHARACTER

This is not about being strong to beat everyone around you but to be a woman who everyone can relate to and take as role model. Whatever she says count in public and her words are not taken lightly. In times of trouble she can be looked up to and her lead can easily be followed by others. She is not selfish and has no negative characteristics around her that put people off. She is able to rebuke in the open with much love than conceal her love for the prideful- thus though she may care where her source of help is coming from at times yet when she has to rebuke, she does it, trusting God for help and putting her confidence only in Him. She is somebody who speaks wisdom and kindness never depart from her tongue.

She opens her mouth in wisdom, and the teaching of kindness is on her tongue. —Proverbs 31:26

She is someone who would rather dress modestly in proper clothing and produce good works than adorn herself with costly garments and pearls and deceive others with her vain beauty and deceitfulness. We would all agree that beauty is easily acquired these days in our beauty stores and anyone can readily become as beautiful as much as they want on the outside. But what you can't find in the supermarkets or anywhere is our inner beauty. The fruit or character we produce will determine what kind of person or woman we are. Therefore she would rather develop and invest in her character building than invest in material things. It is good to dress decently for each occasion but she would not make such things her goal in life. Physical attractiveness is good but it doesn't mean that one is happy or content. Your inner abilities when used positively brings about that expected joy and contentment in oneself.

Woman has a substance which is her power to influence positively or negatively; the positive nature of a woman is first of all embracing who she is and being happy about it. Those who are afraid to be criticized usually bring out the negative side of them which affect them and others negatively.

As a woman you have to be confident in your abilities and should also be honest and straight forward thus being honest about feelings toward others and being straight to talk about them and set boundaries as well as being respectful.

A woman should also be patient with herself and others so that when adversities come she can conquer it and not give up.

A woman should be secured in herself and relationships.

She also plays the role of mother, wife, and girlfriend in a relationship, when she is needed she is there. Moreover she values what she has, a husband, children, work, etc.

There is a saying that behind every successful man there is a woman, if only the woman can possess all these qualities then the saying is true.

INTERESTING TO GET TO KNOW

She does not show all her abilities at once but in every matter and situation she knows and has a way of handling it. Those who get the chance to know her will say she is interesting. People don't get fed up on her and don't give up on her easily. She is not cunning but takes her time carefully to deal with people and situations. She is meek in her deeds and shows a contrite spirit when she falls short or offend others. She allows others to feel more important than herself and she does not seek only for her own interest but others too. There is no selfishness in her; everybody seems equally important to her regardless of their background. She does not strife to please others but work wholeheartedly as she would for the Lord. She does not manipulate others for her greed or show favoritism or be spiteful. In inconsistent times she rises with confident trusting that her courage will influence others to work together for a common goal. Thus in her home, society, work places etc. unplanned events can change our course of direction for good or bad but this woman work over her fears with courage believing that there is an expected end though it might seem that nothing is working well but she perseveres with patience and allow God to take charge. She knows how to appreciate, give thanks and apologize without showing offense or being offended.

OWN DEPTH OF PERSONALITY AND CHARACTER

Oh such a woman who would find? This woman is able to sense wrong and correct it; know what is right and pursue it. She is a person who no matter what would make her right be right and wrong be wrong. An advice from such a person leads to a better future. She knows the right timing to take good chances. She doesn't abuse her power for greed. She doesn't need a stage to stand on or be introduced as a leader to a group of people but everywhere she finds herself she leaves a fragrance of good character for others to emulate. She knows her power and she uses it for good; instead of being a clamorous, foolish woman, she would rather be gracious and retain her honor, build her home than destroy it. She is discreet and careful in her doings. You will never see her quarreling in public yet when she is angered she approaches in a dignified way to settle matters without being self-righteous. She never allows herself to be a snare to others and never tries to bully the weak. Those under her praise her and look forward to seeing her every day. Because of her character and wisdom, people are able to trust her with their own needs and fear. She is able to follow directions from God and her superiors and also cooperate with God's plan for her household. There is honesty and the desire to protect in her be it family or for the love of others. She does not abandon her duties in times of trouble but face it alone or with others even if it means a loss to her. God uses our courage, wisdom, beauty and creativity as useful tools to saves us and others, like He did in Queen Esther's days. (Esther chapter 2 and chapter 4). Because this woman stands out as a lead, her positive character is able to draw out the abilities of others; thus others would want to emulate her so instead of them idling away, they would want to display their abilities too and that is where the woman of substance apply her wisdom by using their strengths as her resources to achieve the goal set. She usually exhibit the servant character than to boss over others yet she is able to maintain her superiority and that is why she is loved by those around her. She intuitively is able to sense beyond others attitudes using clues such as their verbal and nonverbal communications; She is able to read others expressions of emotions and pick out the messages they communicate she mostly calls on past experiences and present realities to solve this kind of issues without alarming the other.

Three

WOMAN AS A WIFE

To be a woman comes with a lot of responsibilities and being a wife is perhaps one of the basic responsibilities of a woman.

A wife is a woman united in lawful wedlock to man and this unity is called marriage, instituted by God himself (Genesis 2:24).

Wife is the crown of her husband (proverbs 12:4). Crown is a glorious object set upon leaders or important people's head to distinguish them from others. Therefore, it is only a husband who can have a wife as a crown upon his head. Mostly, crowns are put on kings' head so that wherever they go they are distinguished from other nations; for instance, an Israelite king from a Moabite king etc.

The crown also commands respect from the home, the community and even distant tribes men.

Wife as a crown over your husband's head, you have to command respect for your husband, from your husband's family, friends, colleagues, tribes' men, nations etc. as a crown, you have to shine on your husband wherever he goes, e.g. in his dressing, his speech and his character.

- Dressing

- Imagine your husband went to an important meeting with you and his hair was not well kept, or two of his buttons in his shirt were not closed or even fallen out, or better still his shoes were not properly lased, and people began watching you and him in an awkward manner how would you feel?

Therefore as a crown on your husband which shines, you have to check his dressing before he goes out.

- As a shining crown, you must look beautiful and graceful at all times in order to appear pleasing and presentable before others thereby commanding respect for your husband. Esther 2:12, 15

Do not think that you don't have money so you will dress anyhow be careful, it can cost you the love of your husband, and reduce you to nothing.

- Speech

Proverbs 16:23—from a wise mind comes wise speech; the words of the wise are persuasive.

As a wife you should not use abusive words on your husband both indoors and outdoors or outside. Remember, the way you speak and the words you use reflect the kind of heart you have, and determine whether it's pure or impure.

Proverbs 22:11—one who loves a pure heart and who speaks with grace will have the king for a friend.

Some women discuss their husbands' issues in public as though their husbands were strangers to them. Be careful! Because doing this make others have the opportunity to make decisions for you which at the long run destroys your home; for all you may know they might even be jealous of you and the little you think you have.

In Esther chapter one, because of queen Vashti's behavior, others made harsh decisions for the women in that town.

A wife needs to master how to speak softly to her husband with much patience and also to master the words I am sorry, please and thank you.

Proverbs 25:15—through patience a ruler can be persuaded, and a gentle tongue can break a bone.

Therefore think about what you would say before speaking wherever you find yourself.

In proverbs as wisdom was attributed to a woman, a wife should be wise in her sayings and conduct to bring honor to herself and her husband.

- Character

Be submissive to your husband everywhere and at all times; this will cause God's favor to be on you wherever you are.

Esther 2:9—she pleased him and won his favor.

Ephesians 5:22—wives, submit yourselves unto your own husbands, as unto the Lord

Proverbs 31:31 talks about the character of a wife

- Virtuous—a wife who possesses virtue and good morals
- Trustworthy—she can be trusted by her husband in many ways e.g. financially, trust her with men, trust her with his children and trust her with his secrets and his weakness
- Has favor from the Lord (proverbs 18:22) so that the husband will always have goodness following him

and no harm on him; this is because she is prayerful
- Hardworking—she cleans the home, able to organize activities, feeds the home and also works a job
- Generous—being able to give to the poor and needy cheerfully
- Appear presentable at all times
- Speaks wisely and give instructions with kindness
- Laziness is not part of her
- She fears the Lord

- A wife as a companion

Another duty of the wife is to be a companion for her husband so that they can spend a lot of time with each other; complement each other.

A wife's companionship comes in the form of –

Friendship—thus two is better than one so one can lift the other's spirit up when the other is down

Comfort—comforting the husband in times of sorrow, grief (Genesis 24:67

Proverbs 16:29

It is also the wife's duty not to lead the husband astray to the wrong path by giving wrong advice.

The wife should not also deprive her husband from having sex because this is also

> *one of her duties. 1 Corinthians 7:5*

And as a wife, it is your duty to procreate; in time of undue delay in child bearing the couple should not hesitate to seek medical attention. But above all they should not overlook their dependence upon God's help in prayers (Psalm 127:3)

> *Proverbs 31:10, 11—an excellent wife who can find? She is far more precious than jewels. The heart of her husband trusts in her, and he will have no lack of gain.*

Don't criticize, nag, and don't lecture but at all times show love in your speech in bringing out the point you want to emphasize.

Proverbs 21:19 better to live in a desert than with a quarrelsome and nagging wife

Proverbs 18:22 says whoso finds a wife, finds a good thing and obtains favor of the lord.

Proverbs 19:14 houses and wealth are inherited from parents, but a prudent wife is from the Lord.

Wives ought to work hard in being understanding and insightful towards their husbands and handle affairs of the house with wisdom; and also bring up the children in an orderly manner.

Furthermore, *proverbs 12:4 says a wife of noble character is her husband's crown, but a disgraceful wife is like decay in his bones.*

With this the wife should not just love but be modest in character and loyal too towards him.

In the other way around, a wife who is weak, lazy, idle, boastful, arrogant and uneconomical, careless is poison to her husband's life, so that he is ashamed to be seen with her, or to be known that he stands in such a relation to her.

This woman is a constant grief to his mind and a pressure upon his spirit.

Four

I read a book which said to have substance is to make meaning, and to add to this fact I always tell people around me "the little things you add up to life makes you stand out and help your blessings come". Many people think they have to do something big to make others notice them but that is not the case.

First of all find a cause outside yourself:

This doesn't mean become a president before you can help solve problems around you. Look into your family, friends, neighborhood and you will notice that there are those who need you more than you could ever imagine. There may be someone who needs help in schooling, job, food, etc.. When you become their source of hope and strength what do you think would happen to them? They will begin to look to you as role model and with faces full of smiles. Instead of giving up, because of you they will not. Are you not bringing out the substance in you? They are the people you would stand for no matter what. Their pain becomes your pain and their joy becomes your joy.

You will improve on the world being a better place:

Who would not be happy to have peace surrounding them, when you do this, you become a source of peace and hope for someone. You teach these people that instead of doing bad and becoming a bad person there is a choice of doing good things and becoming a good person. Imagine, if these good people affect a nation how good do you think the world would be?

You also increase their quality of life:

Their way of thinking and doing things change as well. Although it may at a point feel like without you they can't do anything, your constant advice will sink into their minds one day helping them to know that they can do all things through Christ who strengthens them.

Have you ever met a man who thought his sins would never been forgiven; but then when he had an encounter with this substantial woman he felt very much like he would want to change for good.

As women of power God gave us the ability to foresee what others cannot see and we can use this ability to prevent the end of good things. When good things that keep a family together, neighborhood, or even a nation together are being destroyed by our own people, politicians, or even people who hold other important positions, as women who understand the nurturing power we are able to come together to speak our voice and make our voices heard and most of the time we succeed therefore as a woman of substance with this ability you have, what do you do? You rise up and make your voice heard speaking the truth and bring together solutions that can affect the people positively.

Five

PARTICIPATING ACTIVELY

As women of substance, we participate actively in our daily lives the hardship we go through and how strong we get through the experiences we create. In so doing we become part of the solution and get smarter in our dealings so therefore we are able to make meaning out of life for ourselves and for others too.

This is a courageous woman who is not afraid of failure but take risks and full responsibility for her actions regardless of victory or failure. Her resiliency is able to persist through tough times waiting for her opportunity at the right time and when she finds it she grabs it and make good use of it to bring good results.

She lives by her morals and values which motivates her and energizes her as well as inspires her to do something significant in this world. There are those women who just stand afar and talk about problems around them yet they are scared to take action with the fear of fingers being point at them. But a woman of substance would always stand by the truth and not be afraid of the negative comments she would hear others say about her. To her the solution is more important than the negative thought of others. When she needs to set people straight so they become aware of their wrong actions or sayings, she does that firmly and continues with her goal.

She is able to recognize resources around her either human resources or material resources and used them wisely to achieve her goals. She is not a manipulative person who will try at all cost to do anything to get what she wants; instead she knows when to stop. She is emotionally stable not as though she does not feel stress or pressure but she controls it with prayer and asks for help when needed from reliable sources like her mom or pastor or a reliable friend etc. she is not afraid when others see her weakness but she set a limit as to how much or how far she talks about her problems. She maintains her calm without being aggressive about the problem this helps her choose the right people into her problem for companionship.

Six

WOMAN AS A MOTHER

Mother is a woman who has raised a child, given birth to a child or supplied the egg which in union with a sperm grew into a child. This is the most beautiful experience that a woman can have in her life and sometimes the most stressful.

A mother performs so many tasks in different aspects of her life and for her family.

She takes care of her spouse, children, business, social life and health; yet she has been blessed with the power to handle all this numerous affairs at the same time.

A mother is usually the foundation that a home is built upon

> Providing a home firstly for her husband by procreating and handling the homely affairs like cooking

> She provides safe and secure environment in which the children can grow and flourish and develop their personalities

> She serves as a role model and teaches proper manners to the child since she is the first and closest person the child gets to know.

Proverbs 31:26-27 she opens her mouth with wisdom, and the teaching of kindness is on her tongue. She looks well to the ways of her household and does not eat the bread of idleness.

Isaiah 66:13 as a mother comforts her child, so will I comfort you; and your will be comforted over Jerusalem hid affectionate; when a child hurts him/herself and is crying, she takes him up in her arms, hugs him/her to her bosom and speaks softly and comfortably to him/her to still and quiet the child

Moreover when a mother has an afflicted child or person, she yearns in her heart and does all she can to comfort them

When a child misbehaves, the mother looks shy at the child and carries herself at a distance, which being noticed, the child takes it to heart, and then as it affects the child she returns to the child and comforts the child.

In proverbs 31:25-30 it says strength and honor are her clothing

MAME YAA

A mother shows strength, not through her body but through her mind and therefore able to bear and do all things with a fortitude of mind to withstand every enemy and persevere in well doing.

In times of hardship she purposes in her mind and withstands all hardships that stands in her face and works hard to fend for her children. She is also very protective of her children and families and a disciplinarian and friend too. She works hard to equip her children with knowledge and skills required in life. She makes sure there is a safe environment for her children to live in. She is also their teacher who teaches them important life lessons as they grow up. You are also their confidant who they confide in their time of trouble. Therefore a good mother is one who loves her children, husband, open-minded, accurate, cares for her home and dutiful and kind too.

Seven

In conclusion, a woman of substance is a woman of power who doesn't abuse the power she has but use it for good for the benefit of others and herself. Her capabilities become a set standard for others to emulate. There is no rudeness in her and she is careful in her actions.

Bonus Chapter

Ephesians 4 New
International Version (NIV)

UNITY AND MATURITY IN THE BODY OF CHRIST

⁴ As a prisoner for the Lord, then, I urge you to live a life worthy of the callingyou have received. ² Be completely humble and gentle; be patient, bearing with one another in love. ³ Make every effort to keep the unity of the Spirit through the bond of peace. ⁴ There is one body and one Spirit, just as you were

called to one hope when you were called; ⁵ one Lord, one faith, one baptism; ⁶ one God and Father of all, who is over all and through all and in all.

⁷ But to each one of us grace has been given as Christ apportioned it. ⁸ This is why it[a] says:

"When he ascended on high, he took many captives and gave gifts to his people."[b]

⁹ (What does "he ascended" mean except that he also descended to the lower, earthly regions[c]? ¹⁰ He who descended is the very one who ascended higher than all the heavens, in order to fill the whole universe.) ¹¹ So Christ himself gave the apostles, the prophets, the evangelists, the pastors and teachers, ¹² to equip his people for works of service, so that the body of Christ may be built up ¹³ until we all reach unity in the faith and in the knowledge of the Son of God and become

mature, attaining to the whole measure of the fullness of Christ.

¹⁴ Then we will no longer be infants, tossed back and forth by the waves, and blown here and there by every wind of teaching and by the cunning and craftiness of people in their deceitful scheming. ¹⁵ Instead, speaking the truth in love, we will grow to become in every respect the mature body of him who is the head, that is, Christ. ¹⁶ From him the whole body, joined and held together by every supporting ligament, grows and builds itself up in love, as each part does its work.

Instructions for Christian Living

¹⁷ So I tell you this, and insist on it in the Lord, that you must no longer live as the Gentiles do, in the futility of their

thinking. ⁱ⁸ They are darkened in their understanding and separated from the life of God because of the ignorance that is in them due to the hardening of their hearts. ¹⁹ Having lost all sensitivity, they have given themselves over to sensuality so as to indulge in every kind of impurity, and they are full of greed.

²⁰ That, however, is not the way of life you learned ²¹ when you heard about Christ and were taught in him in accordance with the truth that is in Jesus. ²² You were taught, with regard to your former way of life, to put off your old self, which is being corrupted by its deceitful desires; ²³ to be made new in the attitude of your minds; ²⁴ and to put on the new self, created to be like God in true righteousness and holiness.

²⁵ Therefore each of you must put off falsehood and speak truthfully to your neighbor, for we are all members of one body. ²⁶ "In your anger do not sin"[d]: Do

not let the sun go down while you are still angry, ²⁷ and do not give the devil a foothold. ²⁸ Anyone who has been stealing must steal no longer, but must work, doing something useful with their own hands, that they may have something to share with those in need.

²⁹ Do not let any unwholesome talk come out of your mouths, but only what is helpful for building others up according to their needs, that it may benefit those who listen. ³⁰ And do not grieve the Holy Spirit of God, with whom you were sealed for the day of redemption. ³¹ Get rid of all bitterness, rage and anger, brawling and slander, along with every form of malice. ³² Be kind and compassionate to one another, forgiving each other, just as in Christ God forgave you.

www.ingramcontent.com/pod-product-compliance
Lightning Source LLC
Chambersburg PA
CBHW030134100526
44591CB00009B/660